P R O V E R B S

FROM AROUND THE WORLD

ILLUSTRATED BY

· K A T H Y   D A V I S ·

*To my friends and family for their
support and encouragement. . .
and especially to Ursula for helping me
to believe in my dreams.*

P R O V E R B S

FROM AROUND THE WORLD

The road to a **friend's house** is never long.

I L L U S T R A T E D · B Y

· K A T H Y   D A V I S ·

Great Quotations Publishing Company

Glendale Heights, Illinois • *a division of GREAT QUOTATIONS, INC.*

The sources from which these proverbs were taken have
not been acknowledged, as they are often attributable to
more than one source and appear in many variations.

Published in the United States by
Great Quotations Publishing Co.
**1967 Quincy Court, Glendale Heights
Illinois 60139 - 2045**
Color Separations by Graphics 2000, Westmont, IL

Printed in Hong Kong

ISBN 1-56245-017-4

1   2   3   4   5   6   7   8   9   10

Printing/AK/Year   97   96   95   94   93   92   91

INTRODUCTION

"A short saying often contains much wisdom."
— Sophocles

The wisdom of the ages has been collected from around the world and celebrated in color by the wonderful art and calligraphy of Kathy Davis.

A proverb is a short saying, full of infinite knowledge that has been handed down from generation to generation. Though many of the proverbs reflect the national character of its origin, each saying has universal appeal. Often amusing, the proverbs are rich in imagery. They can be appreciated for their literal impression as well as on a deeper level for their profound meaning.

The sources from which these proverbs have been gathered are not mentioned, as they are derived from many references, often appearing in different variations.

Combining age-old proverbs with colorful and contemporary artwork, the *Book of Proverbs* is a treasure of international humor and insight.

5

When an
ELEPHANT
is in trouble,
even a
FROG
will kick him.

·HINDU PROVERB·

Small children don't let
you sleep; big children
don't let you rest.

YIDDISH PROVERB

Everyone must row with
the oars he has.

ENGLISH PROVERB

A wise man changes his
mind, a fool never will.

SPANISH PROVERB

If all pulled in one direction, the world would keel over.

YIDDISH PROVERB

The silent dog is the first to bite.

GERMAN PROVERB

No man is so tall that he never need stretch and none so small that he never need stoop.

DANISH PROVERB

In a
GOOD APPLE
you sometimes
find a
worm.

· Y I D D I S H   P R O V E R B ·

It is better
to
light a candle
than to
curse the darkness

· C H I N E S E   P R O V E R B ·

Govern a family as you
would cook a small fish —
very gently.

CHINESE PROVERB

It is a long lane that has
no turning.

ENGLISH PROVERB

A single arrow is easily
broken, but not ten
in a bundle.

JAPANESE PROVERB

**If you're out to beat a dog,
you're sure to find a stick.**

YIDDISH PROVERB

**Try to reason about
love, and you will lose
your reason.**

FRENCH PROVERB

**He who digs a hole for
another may fall in
himself.**

RUSSIAN PROVERB

All is not

cream

that comes
from a cow.

· YIDDISH PROVERB ·

When the
MOUSE
laughs at the
CAT,
there is a hole
nearby.

· NIGERIAN PROVERB ·

Hold a true friend with
both your hands.

NIGERIAN PROVERB

Big mouthfuls often choke.

ITALIAN PROVERB

A broken hand works, but
not a broken heart.

PERSIAN PROVERB

**Measure a thousand times
and cut once.**

TURKISH PROVERB

**You don't water a camel
with a spoon.**

ARMENIAN PROVERB

**To be a parent takes
knowhow, but everyone
takes it on anyhow.**

YIDDISH PROVERB

Coffee
should be
black as hell
strong as death
and sweet as love

· TURKISH PROVERB ·

**Not to know is bad; not to
wish to know is worse.**

NIGERIAN PROVERB

One can't fill a torn sack.

YIDDISH PROVERB

**The best mirror is an
old friend.**

GERMAN PROVERB

The
FROG
tried to look
as big as the
ELEPHANT
and burst.

. A F R I C A N   P R O V E R B .

One cannot manage
too many affairs;
like
Pumpkins
in the water,
one pops up while you try to
hold down the other

· CHINESE PROVERB ·

The loftiest towers rise
from the ground.

CHINESE PROVERB

— ● —

Men count up the faults of
those who keep them
waiting.

FRENCH PROVERB

— ● —

He who lets the small
things bind him leaves the
great undone behind him.

SCANDINAVIAN PROVERB

After all,
to make a
beautiful omelet
you have to

BREAK AN EGG

·SPANISH PROVERB·

To fall down you manage
alone but it takes friendly
hands to get up.

YIDDISH PROVERB

That is a bad bridge that is
shorter than the stream.

GERMAN PROVERB

If you run after two
rabbits, you won't catch
either one.

ARMENIAN PROVERB

If you sit in a hot bath, you
think the whole town
is warm.

YIDDISH PROVERB

If you try to cleanse others,
you will waste away, like
soap, in the process.

MADAGASCAN PROVERB

The morning is wiser than
the evening.

RUSSIAN PROVERB

A
PIG
grabs the
best apple.

·YIDDISH PROVERB·

**Everybody knows good
counsel except him that
has need of it.**

GERMAN PROVERB

**If you are reluctant to ask
the way, you will be lost.**

MALAYSIAN PROVERB

**You do not really know
your friends from your
enemies until the
ice breaks.**

ICELANDIC PROVERB

A
Teacher
is
better than
two books.

If a little tree grows in the
shade of a larger tree, it
will die small.

SENEGALESE PROVERB

There's no one as deaf as
he who will not listen.

YIDDISH PROVERB

He that conceals his grief
finds no remedy for it.

TURKISH PROVERB

It is good everywhere, but
home is better.

YIDDISH PROVERB

• ■ •

Wisdom and virtue are like
the two wheels of a cart.

JAPANESE PROVERB

• ■ •

One cannot ski so
softly that the traces
cannot be seen.

FINNISH PROVERB

Danger
and
Delight
grow on
one stalk.

· ENGLISH PROVERB ·

The noisiest drum has
nothing in it but air.

ENGLISH PROVERB

The arrow that has left the
bow never returns.

PERSIAN PROVERB

A prudent man does not
make the goat his
gardener.

HUNGARIAN PROVERB

A drowning man is not
troubled by rain.

PERSIAN PROVERB

A life without love is like a
year without summer.

SWEDISH PROVERB

If the camel once gets his
nose in the tent, his body
will soon follow.

ARABIC PROVERB

TRUST IN GOD,

but tie
your camel.

· PERSIAN PROVERB ·

**The liar is not believed
even when he tells
the truth.**

YIDDISH PROVERB

**That which is loved is
always beautiful.**

NORWEGIAN PROVERB

**The camel does not see
his own hump.**

ARMENIAN PROVERB

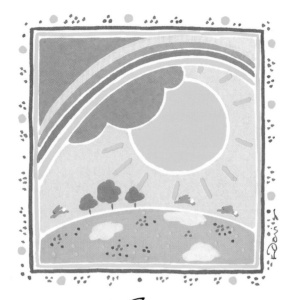

The
Sun
shines brighter
after a
shower.

· YIDDISH PROVERB ·

If you want to please everybody, you'll die before your time.

YIDDISH PROVERB

A young branch takes on all the bends that one gives it.

CHINESE PROVERB

When spider webs unite, they can tie up a lion.

ETHIOPIAN PROVERB

**Don't judge any man until
you have walked two
moons in his moccasins.**

AMERICAN INDIAN PROVERB

**No one tests the depth of a
river with both feet.**

ASHANTI PROVERB

**Every way up has
its way down.**

YIDDISH PROVERB

GOD GIVES

every bird its food
but does not always
drop it into the nest.

· D A N I S H   P R O V E R B ·

He who would make a fool
of himself finds many to
help him.

DANISH PROVERB

Many seek good nights and
lose good days.

DUTCH PROVERB

In the ant's house, the
dew is a flood.

AFGHANISTAN PROVERB

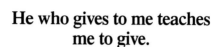

He who gives to me teaches
me to give.

DANISH PROVERB

A guest sees more in an
hour than the host
in a year.

POLISH PROVERB

I dance to the tune that
is played.

SPANISH PROVERB

He who builds to
everyman's

advice

will have a
crooked house

· D A N I S H   P R O V E R B ·

He who is no good to
himself is no good
to another.

YIDDISH PROVERB

There are none so blind as
they that won't see.

ENGLISH PROVERB

One arrow does not bring
down two birds.

TURKISH PROVERB

WORRIES
go down better
with soup
than
without

· YIDDISH PROVERB ·

**He who likes his work, to
him work comes easy.**

YIDDISH PROVERB

**He who is being carried
does not realize how far the
town is.**

NIGERIAN PROVERB

**Children are a poor
man's riches.**

ENGLISH PROVERB

The comforter's head
never aches.

ITALIAN PROVERB

Patience, and the mulberry
leaf become a silk gown.

CHINESE PROVERB

Pride in children is more
precious than money.

YIDDISH PROVERB

He
FISHES
on.
who catches

one.

· FRENCH PROVERB ·

A baby is an angel who's
wings decrease as his
legs increase.

FRENCH PROVERB

What breaks in a moment
may take years to mend.

SWEDISH PROVERB

What the wind brings, it
will also take away.

ARMENIAN PROVERB

**A rich child often sits on a
poor mother's lap.**

DANISH PROVERB

**The best brewer sometimes
makes bad beer.**

GERMAN PROVERB

**Nothing is so burdensome
as a secret.**

FRENCH PROVERB

Don't
SAIL
out farther than
you can
ROW
back.

· DANISH PROVERB ·

**When a toothache comes,
you forget your headache.**

YIDDISH PROVERB

**If you don't crack the
shell, you can't eat the nut.**

RUSSIAN PROVERB

**To be willing is only half
the task.**

ARMENIAN PROVERB

Don't give me any
honey
and spare me the
sting.

·YIDDISH PROVERB·

**The best horse needs a
whip and the smartest
person needs advice.**

YIDDISH PROVERB

**He who is shipwrecked the
second time cannot lay the
blame on Neptune.**

ENGLISH PROVERB

**Truth and oil always come
to the surface.**

SPANISH PROVERB

Between saying and doing
many a pair of shoes is
worn out.

ITALIAN PROVERB

Talk does not cook rice.

CHINESE PROVERB

Everyone is kneaded out of
the same dough but not
baked in the same oven.

YIDDISH PROVERB

Every
path
has its
puddle.

· ENGLISH PROVERB ·

Only the wearer knows where the shoe pinches.

ENGLISH PROVERB

Worry often gives a small thing a big shadow.

SWEDISH PROVERB

Who begins too much accomplishes little.

GERMAN PROVERB

**Men trip not on
mountains, they stumble
on stones.**

HINDUSTANI PROVERB

Rust wastes more than use.

FRENCH PROVERB

**Tasty is the fish from
someone else's table.**

YIDDISH PROVERB

THE CRAB

instructs its young
" Walk straight ahead
— like me."

·HINDUSTANI PROVERB·

I murmured because I had
no shoes, until I met a man
who had no feet.

PERSIAN PROVERB

Confidence is half
the victory.

YIDDISH PROVERB

You may go where you
wish, but you cannot
escape yourself.

NORWEGIAN PROVERB

If I drown in a pond, it is an ocean to me.

ARMENIAN PROVERB

Every day cannot be a feast of lanterns.

CHINESE PROVERB

Patience is a bitter plant but it has sweet fruit.

GERMAN PROVERB

It is only
the
first bottle
that is
expensive

· FRENCH PROVERB ·

Don't try to fly before you
have wings.

FRENCH PROVERB

He who once burnt his
mouth always blows
his soup.

GERMAN PROVERB

Don't throw away the old
bucket until you're sure the
new one holds water.

SWEDISH PROVERB

**He who would leap high
must take a long run.**

DANISH PROVERB

**One of these days is none
of these days.**

ENGLISH PROVERB

**The sun will set without
your assistance.**

YIDDISH PROVERB

The road to a
friend's house
is never
long.

·DANISH · PROVERB·

ABOUT THE ARTIST

Kathy Davis is an artist whose creative efforts include illustration and greeting card design. Her interest in painting, calligraphy, research and writing have led her, naturally, to the book and gift industries. Kathy's joy in the creative process is reflected in her upbeat and contemporary style. Her work may be described as fresh, colorful and expressive. Her book of proverbs combines inspiration and humor, giving a refreshing look to age old wisdom.

A diverse background as an art educator, painter and graphic artist has brought great variety to her work, which always reflects a distinctively personal style.

Kathy lives outside of Philadelphia with her two children, Ben and Katie.